Motherland Sweet Motherland

written and illustrated by

Antoinette Brooks

For my beautiful mother, who inspired me with tales of her Jamaican childhood all those years ago. Oh, how I loved listening to her and my aunts reminiscing about life "back home."

Text copyright © 2022 by Antoinette Brooks
Illustrations copyright © 2022 by Antoinette Brooks

All Rights Reserved. No part of this publication, or the characters within it, may be reproduced or distributed in any form or by any means without permission of the publisher or author in writing.

ISBN: 978-1-915539-01-4

Bright Thoughts Publishing

MissBrooksLovesBooks.com

This book belongs to

....

Sun bursts bright on idle sky.
Rooster screams his morning cry.

Fetch mop and broom to do our chores.
Find eggs and firewood, sweep outdoors.

School bell ringing far away.
"We must not be late," we say.

Motherland, sweet Motherland,
my heart beats strong and true.
Motherland, sweet Motherland,
my heart belongs to you.

Schoolyard laughter, cousins and friends.
We walk home playing when school day ends.

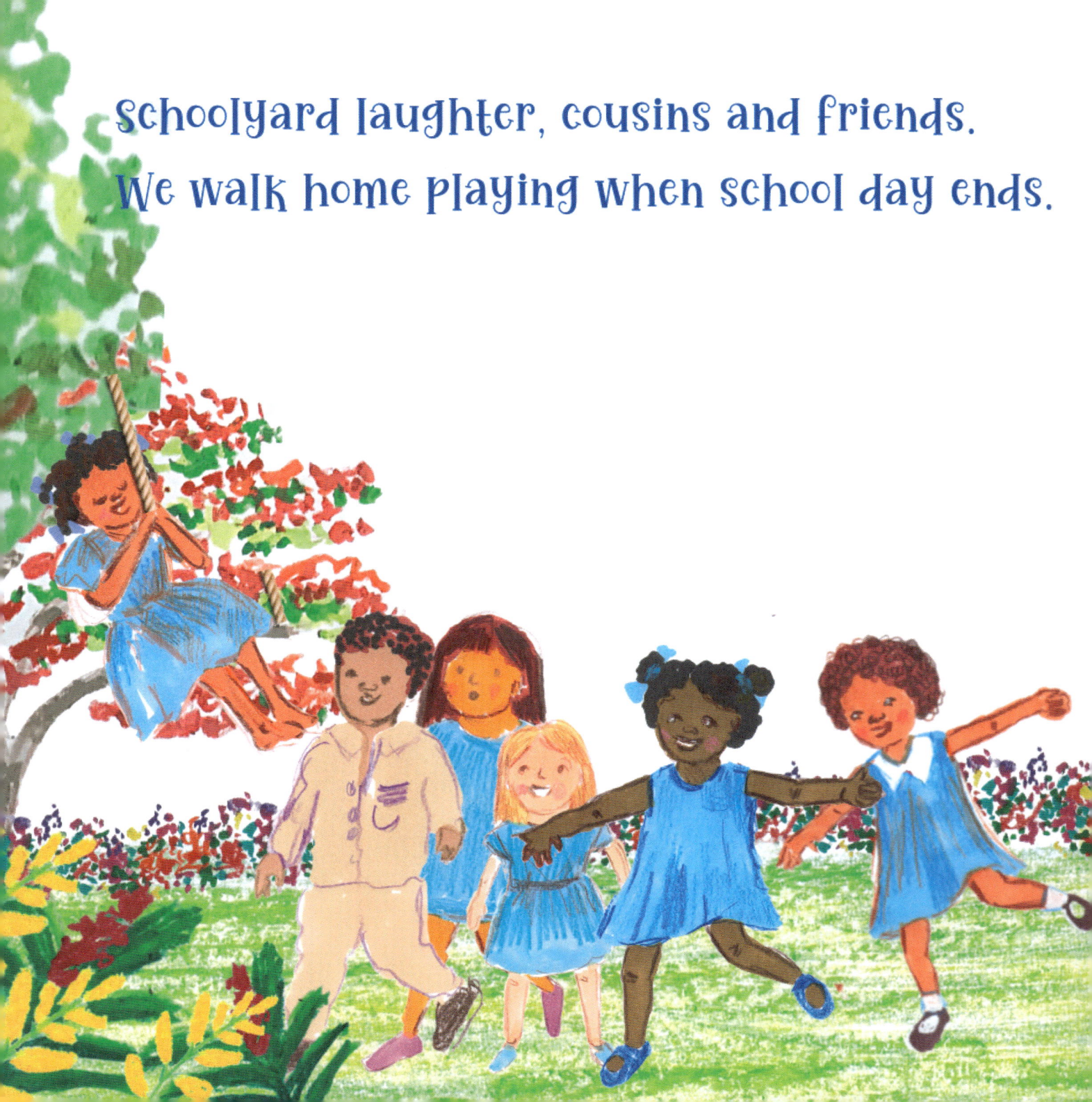

Motherland, sweet Motherland,
my heart beats strong and true.
Motherland, sweet Motherland,
how I long for you.

Grandma on verandah, rocking style.
Neighbours call, "Momma," and chat awhile.

Uncle Baada, home from cutting cane, plays his fife while we dance and game.

Motherland, sweet Motherland,
my heart beats strong and true.
Motherland, sweet Motherland,
how I long for you.

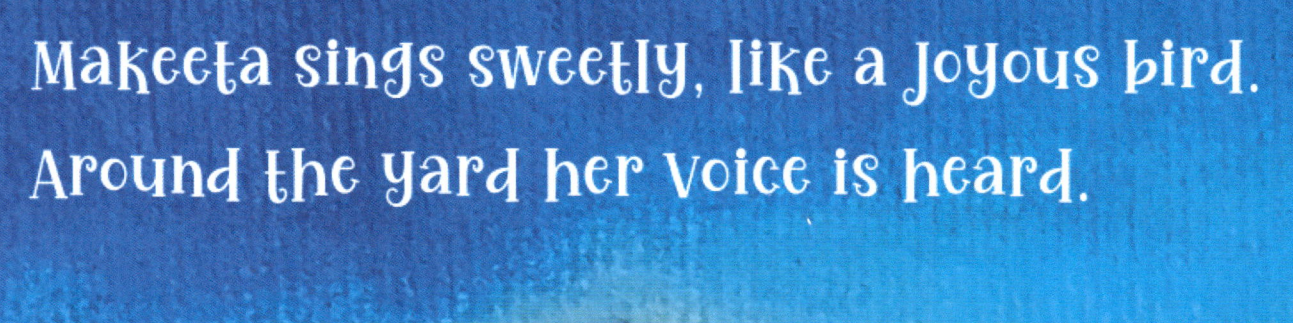

Makeeta sings sweetly, like a joyous bird.
Around the yard her voice is heard.

Motherland, sweet Motherland,
my heart beats strong and true.
Motherland, sweet Motherland,
how I still miss you.

We are late with dinner for cross Uncle Pen.
He takes the pots and shuts his door again.

Motherland, sweet Motherland,
my heart beats strong and true.
Motherland, sweet Motherland,
how I long for you.

Dasheen, plaintain, bami, yam.
Time to chatter, time to nyam*.

Motherland, sweet Motherland,
my heart beats strong and true
Motherland, sweet Motherland,
how I still miss you.

*Caribbean word for eat.

Aunt Mamidear orders us to bed. We say prayers and climb under the pretty spread.

Motherland, sweet Motherland, my heart beats strong and true. Motherland, sweet Motherland, how I long for you.

Moon shines bright so large and high,
until sun bursts bright on idle sky.

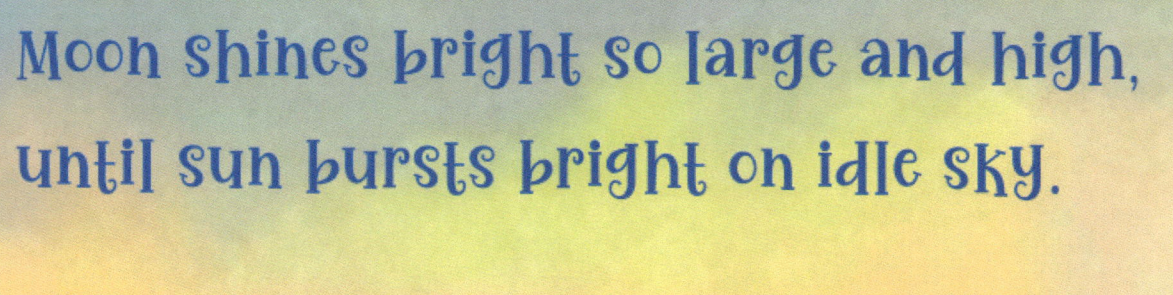

Motherland, sweet Motherland,
my heart beats strong and true.
Motherland, sweet Motherland,
forever and always, I will long for you.

Dear Reader

Thank you so much for reading! The words, about that eternal longing for comfort and that idyllic sense of home, came from my heart.

I hope you loved this story. Please do leave a review for me. It makes such a difference and really helps me to share these stories with more readers.

Get Exclusive Motherland, Sweet Motherland

I love writing and sharing my stories with you!

Join my Readers' Club for freebies, news on upcoming books and exclusive content in the Startup Library, including **FREE** content on Motherland, Sweet Motherland.

Just visit **www.MissBrooksLovesBooks.com**

About the Author

Antoinette Brooks loved creating stories and scribbling pictures from an early age. She studied Economics at the University of London, before realising she was a hopeless economist who did not care for maths or figures, and much preferred words and drawing instead.

About this book she says, "My parents came from rural Jamaica, and I loved hearing the stories of everyday life that my mother and aunt shared with me. Those were wonderful days and times. I treasure all the memories and it is my joy to share some of them with you!"

Other Books by Antoinette Brooks

For younger readers, the Tippy Tappy Katkins series

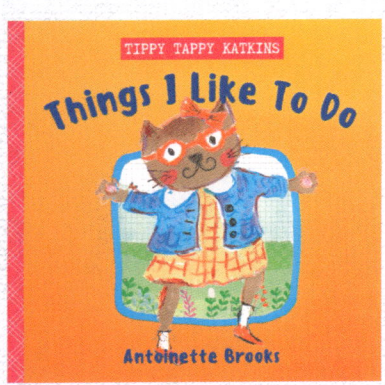

Things I Like to Do

Meet the wonderful Tippy Tappy and discover all the different things she likes to do.

A fun, interactive book for early learners.

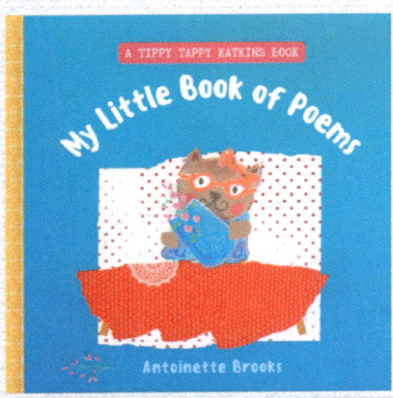

My Little Book of Poems

Coming Soon!

Tippy Tappy has a book of little poems which younger readers will love!

Printed in Great Britain
by Amazon